MANAGING DIVERSITY AND
THE BUS

Mustafa F.

Gary Mulho

Ahu Tatli

Dianah Wo

The Chartered Institute of Personnel and Development is the leading publisher of books and reports for personnel and training professionals, students, and all those concerned with the effective management and development of people at work.
For full details of all our titles, please contact the Publishing Department:
Tel: 020 8612 6204
E-mail: publish@cipd.co.uk

To view and purchase all CIPD titles:
www.cipd.co.uk/bookstore

For details of CIPD research projects:
www.cipd.co.uk/research

MANAGING DIVERSITY AND THE BUSINESS CASE

Mustafa F. Özbilgin

NORWICH BUINESS SCHOOL, UNIVERSITY OF EAST ANGLIA

Gary Mulholland

YORK ST JOHN UNIVERSITY

Ahu Tatli

SCHOOL OF BUSINESS AND MANAGEMENT, QUEEN MARY COLLEGE, UNIVERSITY OF LONDON

Dianah Worman

CHARTERED INSTITUTE OF PERSONNEL AND DEVELOPMENT

First published 2008
Reprinted 2009

Cover and text design by Sutchinda Rangsi-Thompson
Typeset by Paperweight
Printed in Great Britain by Short Run Press, Exeter

British Library Cataloguing in Publication Data
A catalogue record for this book is available from the British Library

ISBN-13   978 1 84398 223 4

Chartered Institute of Personnel and Development,
151 The Broadway, London SW19 1JQ

Tel: 020 8612 6200
Website: www.cipd.co.uk

Incorporated by Royal Charter. Registered charity no. 1079797.

CONTENTS

Acknowledgements · viii

Foreword · ix

Executive summary · xi

1 **Introduction** · 1

2 **Diversity management and the link with business performance** · 3

3 **The business case for diversity – how prevalent is it in practice?** · 9

4 **The business case for diversity – how much difference is it making?** · 13

5 **Driving diversity progress – how much power do those in the driving seat have?** · 17

6 **Managing diversity better – making more of what we know** · 21

7 **The business case for diversity – what action research shows us** · 25

8 **Pepping up the pace of progress – some ideas** · 31

References · 33

ACKNOWLEDGEMENTS

The CIPD is very grateful to all those organisations and individuals who gave their time to take part in the State of the Nation survey, the Diversity Action Research Network. We should also offer our special thanks to individuals and organisations who have contributed to this report in other ways.

FOREWORD

During the first half of 2008 conversations babbled that the 'credit crunch' could damage the progress of diversity. The gloomy prognosis predicted that diversity had had its day and was doomed.

This negative view lays down the gauntlet to those who wish to defend managing diversity and provide evidence of its importance in sustaining high-performance working.

A CIPD diversity conference in May 2008 featured testimonies from organisations that have embedded diversity into everything they do. They continue to 'red thread' it in all activities – not just people management and development policies and practices – because they see that diversity should be viewed as an enabler to cope with stiff commercial competition, not an administrative overhead.

The tough global economic climate emerging at the time of going to press, as well as pending changes regarding UK discrimination law, makes this report timely – in refreshing understanding about the *business case* for diversity and its relevance for influencing change and adding value.

Using information drawn from a range of different and unique research studies that we carried out to explore the business case for managing diversity, we describe its inclusive nature, how it can add value to business performance and how it differentiates leading-edge diversity organisations from the followers: those who are essentially preoccupied with legal compliance.

We show how managing diversity is a dynamic process and a way of doing things, rather than a collection of discrete initiatives. We provide evidence that the main business driver for managing diversity is currently the need to tackle the global 'war for talent'. This leaves huge potential for organisations to add even more value to business performance by paying more attention to a range of other recognised business drivers as well.

The evidence we have gained from the various research studies undertaken shows that the preoccupation with compliance, limited understanding about the nature of the business case and underinvestment in resources (in terms of specific diversity budgets and expertise to drive change) all prevent organisations from maintaining momentum on managing diversity and driving it to the heart of business activity. This can make managing diversity superficial and less capable of making an impact and fuels doubt about its relevance to the bottom line.

Our work shows that for managing diversity to have a higher profile in the UK, public awareness-raising is vital, making it clear that managing diversity is about inclusion and goes beyond issues covered by discrimination legislation. It is certainly not about exclusion and should not marginalise people who cannot be 'labelled' according to law. Rather it is about everybody because everyone is different. This will improve knowledge and understanding and stimulate employer engagement. It should be based on making information about the business case for managing diversity coherent and robust and the provision of easily accessible practical guidance to remove the fear and paralysis that the focus on compliance feeds on.

Organisations need more than information about their legal obligations. They need case study examples of evolving good practice, practical tools to help them craft contextually appropriate business cases for action, a facility to help them interact with others striving to make managing diversity central to all business activity and access to people with diversity expertise. Such help and support needs to be made available through a one-stop, well-signposted helpline with links to good-quality, reliable websites, for example those of the Equality and Human Rights Commission (EHRC), the CIPD, the Trades Union Congress (TUC), and so on.

The model that supports the Government's Age Postive initiative and the reputable Acas helpline are excellent building blocks for such an information and support facility, but the challenge is how to improve and continue to improve the provision of quality information, help and support, for which we see a growing appetite.

In our view key stakeholders and authorities in the management of diversity should be encouraged by the Government to work in partnership to share knowledge, understanding, perspectives and experiences and learn from each other rather than focusing on reinventing wheels – time is too short for this. Such players need to be encouraged to be two-way communication brokers to get messages about managing diversity down to the grassroots of their own constituencies where actions can have a real impact – and capture learning about what works and what does not and why. This information should be captured and fed back to policy-makers and information providers to update and re-inform practical guidance.

It is clear from the extensive research carried out by the CIPD that far more work is needed to inform good practice to facilitate the progress of diversity. And, we predict that it will continue to be needed as organisations progress the diversity agenda and expose yet more challenges and uncharted territories.

Managing diversity is a pervasive issue that touches most activities in business. Far from diversity experts or champions aspiring to work themselves out of a job by helping everyone to see how it is relevant to what they do, they will need to be helped to be expert change agents, influencers and engines to power up progress on a continuous basis and keep the momentum going.

Our research and experience throws up the need for more research to be done to identify the kinds of top-team leadership behaviours that will affect the organisational culture change those working in the diversity field recognise as vital to enable diversity benefits to flourish.

It is also clear that we need to spell out how diversity is relevant to issues such as talent management, total reward management, work–life balance and flexibility, branding, performance management, acquisition management, well-being, mentoring, learning and training, and so on, as the connections don't seem to be automatically made.

We need to understand diversity issues not covered by law much better than we do, for example, generational diversity.

Regarding behaviour, we need to improve the design of interventions to foster respect and dignity in the workplace and the removal of all forms of intimidation, which has a deleterious effect on individual and business performance. We also need to identify the kinds of positive and desirable behaviours we should nurture to create an open, creative workplace. We can't afford to limit our attentions to the negative behaviours we need to stamp out, but neither can we ignore them.

This is a huge but not exhaustive list of issues for attention. But it is a truism that the more you know about managing diversity the more you realise how little you know. As already made clear, managing diversity is not a series of discrete initiatives. It is a dynamic process capable of building quality into all business practices, addressing the circumstances businesses operate in, the people employed to deliver goals and objectives and the customers and clients organisations aim to please and satisfy to be successful entities.

The evidence we have gained from the CIPD research on diversity shows that ignoring diversity is dangerous. Behaving like an ostrich – burying your head in the sand – is to deny opportunities to sustain competitive advantage. Rather than shying away from managing diversity, organisations need to find the courage to go for it.

The CIPD's future research programme for 2008–09 includes studies on generational diversity and a focus on respect and dignity and leadership behaviours.

Based on the learning from the CIPD research findings on managing diversity and the business case, an interactive practical tool has been designed for CIPD members to help them develop a business case for appropriate action in their organisations. Entitled *How to build your own business case for diversity and inclusion*, it is available on the CIPD's website [www.cipd.co.uk/subjects].

Additionally, to facilitate learning about the practical challenges organisations face in progressing diversity and to inform the CIPD's diversity research agenda and public policy positions on diversity, a Senior Diversity Network has been set up. This learning and thought-leadership forum of senior experienced professionals in managing diversity provides a rich opportunity for the Institute and the Forum members to exchange information, experience, thoughts and ideas and take into account research findings to consolidate and develop new thinking about good practice.

For more information about CIPD materials on managing diversity, see the References section of this report.

Dianah Worman, OBE, Chartered FCIPD
CIPD Adviser, Diversity

EXECUTIVE SUMMARY

A rigorous review of hard evidence reveals that diversity management makes business sense and has the potential to contribute to better business performance.

This is the conclusion from a raft of research on managing diversity in the UK undertaken over the last decade by the Chartered Institute of Personnel and Development (CIPD) using various research methods to

❖ investigate and assess the evidence related to the business case

❖ find out if and why organisations value diversity

❖ find out what generic progress has been made

❖ scope methods and tools for measuring diversity

❖ produce good practice guidance and practical tips to help employers implement change and make progress by translating rhetorical arguments and words into actions.

This report reflects on and synthesises various evidence about managing diversity including fresh evidence from various CIPD findings. This evidence includes a five-year CIPD action research project in which nine public, private and voluntary sector organisations took part, case studies, a literature review and a unique CIPD survey on the state of the nation regarding managing diversity, as well as general developments in the field of managing diversity and other academic studies.

Despite the overwhelming evidence that diversity makes business sense, the CIPD national survey shows that organisations in the UK are failing to make the full use of

the potential that diversity management offers – as there is a gap between this evidence and the way managing diversity is practised.

Organisations can close this gap and gain more benefits from managing diversity by making it central to business progress through:

❖ giving attention to the diverse needs and preferences of people as employees, customers and clients so that it becomes a coherent business issue

❖ planning, implementing, monitoring, assessing and revising effective strategies for managing diversity in ways which contribute to organisational goals, performance targets and strategies

❖ aligning diversity management and business strategy to capitalise on diversity related opportunities

❖ taking advantage of the different drivers for progressing diversity which include those related to business, legal, social and moral arguments

❖ effecting progress by recognising and rewarding good practice and the achievement of diversity goals

❖ promoting diversity by showcasing, advocating and supporting work that is done.

A CIPD executive briefing, *Diversity management: words into actions*, includes a range of examples to show how organisations can make diversity integral to their business activities, and another, *Managing diversity in practice: supporting business goals,* includes various case studies to show how organisations customise what they do to deliver success.

These reports show how organisations can use both subtle approaches and more structured and transformational change initiatives to tailor how they incorporate diversity into what they do to support business goals.

Taking the focus away from organisation-specific progress in managing diversity to supporting more generic progress, this report highlights how academic–practitioner collaboration can encourage academic advances in diversity management to influence, inform and support diversity policy and good practice developments.

In our experience academic–practitioner collaboration in the field of managing diversity can lead to the design of more sophisticated and focused approaches to organisational progress based on evident links between diversity management and business performance.

The range of academic–practitioner collaboration described in this report includes partnerships between academics and diversity practitioners, trainers, consultants, advocates, champions and policy-makers.

An examination of the processes and tenets of academic–practitioner collaboration shows that tacit and explicit knowledge transfers can support the design of practical ways of implementing and achieving benefits from managing diversity and the development of academic knowledge and theories. Collaboration enables academics to provide organisations and practitioners with robust evidence-based insights to apply and test in real situations.

To achieve successful outcomes from academic–practitioner collaboration we have designed an action research method based on our experiences of carrying out the CIPD diversity action research programme. This report describes how we designed and applied an action research method to build new knowledge about managing diversity which in our view could be more widely adopted to speed up diversity progress.

INTRODUCTION

This report explores the business case for managing diversity and draws on various research evidence to show the links with performance improvement including:

✧ academic literature

✧ anecdotal case studies

✧ CIPD action research

✧ a unique CIPD national electronic survey showing the state of the nation on diversity management.

The report points out that while the main business case arguments for managing diversity focus on organisational (micro) level issues, clear business case arguments also exist at the national (macro), and personal and professional (meso) levels. Adding all these together shows the real importance of managing diversity and the integral links it has in terms of performance generally. Managing diversity can help to shape, influence and inform the better design and delivery of products and services to diverse societies and deliver improvements to the quality of life for everyone through increased personal choice and opportunities to be economically independent.

Despite a range of convincing evidence, reasoned arguments, and evolving regulation about diversity there continues to be a gap between rhetoric and reality. Far more resources need to be invested in the provision of information and guidance about how to design ways of improving performance through good practice and how to show what added value it can make. The CIPD has set out ideas about measurement to track the impact of diversity practice in a survey report called *Diversity in business: a focus for progress* (2007), in which both quantitative and qualitative techniques are discussed as ways of making diversity progress more transparent.

Based on the CIPD's experience of carrying out action research on making diversity progress, it is clear that more academic–practitioner collaboration could help to improve knowledge and expertise and provide evidence-based approaches to deliver successful outcomes. It is therefore recommended as a way of helping to build new knowledge to speed up the progress of managing diversity.

DIVERSITY MANAGEMENT AND THE LINK WITH BUSINESS PERFORMANCE

❖ **An inspection of the business case for managing diversity using various research methods, points in the same direction – there is one.**

❖ **As shown in the CIPD executive briefing, *Diversity: stacking up the evidence* (2003), there is extensive academic literature on the causal link between the effective management of diversity and business success. However this evidence is patchy in terms of the diversity issues covered and the perspectives taken about performance measures.**

The evidence shows there are elements to the business case for diversity that go beyond the more narrow focus that generally prevails in practice and that better ways of tracking the impact that managing diversity can deliver to performance improvements will make the existing business case arguments more powerful.

The CIPD has set out the main elements of the 'business case' for diversity in its core free guide, *Managing diversity: people make the difference at work but everyone is different* (2005), and makes it clear that the main elements include:

❖ customer care and marketplace competitiveness

❖ corporate image, brand, ethics and values

❖ recruitment and retention of talent

❖ designing and delivering products and services

❖ increasing creativity and innovation

❖ being an employer of choice through effective people management and development

❖ complying with legislation

❖ corporate social responsibility.

The main arguments and drivers related to these elements are explored in the CIPD's state of the nation survey reports, *Diversity in business: how much progress have employers made?* (2006) and *Diversity in business: a focus for progress.*(2007).

FROM EQUALITY TO DIVERSITY TO INCLUSION

Over the last three of four decades much has changed about the way unfair discrimination and exclusion are addressed.

This evolution has taken place against the background of new thinking about the implications of a person being *different*. This new way of thinking about diversity is gradually changing the prevailing negative perceptions about difference causing problems to recognising that difference offers opportunities – bringing new ideas and perspectives about ways of doing things and answers to challenges.

This evolved thinking about the value of difference is taking place against growing social and political acceptance of the importance of tackling unfair discrimination for moral, social and economic reasons, and the need for public policy provisions and social interventions and business activities to be based on *inclusion* to reflect the needs, aspirations and expectations of an increasingly diverse society and diverse global market place.

The more recent developments about diversity have sprung from the acceptance of the need to protect people against unfair discrimination based on ethnicity, gender and disability by giving them legal rights to take complaints through the courts to get redress and compensation.

But commentators (for example, Cockburn, 1991) have challenged the effectiveness of law in delivering significant change because of inadequate levels of legal compliance.

And, in terms of equality of opportunity for everyone regarding jobs and training, CIPD evidence drawn from a unique national level survey on the state of the nation on diversity management (published in the two reports referred to above), provided clear evidence that while law is a key driver for tackling unfair discrimination, it is not enough to deliver the progress that is needed to create an inclusive society and equality.

In the mid 1990s, the concept of diversity management developed and drew attention away from legal compliance. It focused on the strategic value of diversity across a wider range of personal characteristics than were covered by law at the time, which were essentially gender, ethnicity, and disability. Issues now covered by law that were known to cause unfair treatment, for example, age, sexual orientation, religion and spiritual belief, were given a focus in terms of business case reasons for the development of good practice to achieve more inclusivity.

Others issues not covered by law, such as weight, accent, social class and educational background also began to be recognised as potential causes of unfair exclusion from jobs and training as well as goods and services.

Diversity management is based on the premise that everyone is a unique and complex mix of different personal characteristics. It is not based on the assumption that everyone is exactly the same and must therefore be treated in a uniform way, but it does recognise that people have things in common with each other and that these things create group identities.

The fact that people are the same, but different, means that responses to diversity that are based on treating everyone in exactly the same way in relation to perceptions about group norms or a group label or identity, fail to recognise true individuality and responses to personal preferences, needs and choices, and can therefore be argued to be *exclusive* and unfair. In effect, it holds back on difference over and above what is regarded as normal. It caps what is perceived to be beyond what is comparatively normal while it compensates for anything that is perceived to be less than comparatively normal.

The use of a comparator model informed by group norms therefore, falls far short of what is needed to deliver inclusion for everyone regarding economic independence and access to goods and services. People need different kinds of provisions, help and support even to reach the much espoused level playing field associated with equality of opportunity. As an aspirational goal, this is in effect a default position. It stops people going beyond what is regarded as normal and reaching their full individual potential and inhibits marketplace provisions and services which address niche requirements.

In this way the true celebration of difference is blocked as it cuts off the positive aspects of difference and focuses on the negative aspects using a compensation model to make up for any shortcomings in what is regarded as *fair*. This approach itself acts as a barrier to the full potential that a focus on celebrating diversity can deliver as a source of new insights, perspectives and opportunities. These can help to build improvements in the way organisations run their businesses and deliver better designed products and services to reach more diverse audiences and societies effectively and efficiently.

So a new approach to the agenda of managing diversity is needed to support the new thinking or mindset about diversity and inclusion.

Key and highly provocative is the need to reposition the vexed issue of 'positive discrimination'.

To date the UK regulatory framework for tackling unfair discrimination has positioned positive discrimination as unlawful while positive action is permissible within certain constraints. (Positive action is aimed at encouraging job applications from more diverse groups in the labour market or enabling people from under-represented groups to take part in specially designed exclusive training to help them compete for jobs more successfully).

To explain the concept of positive discrimination more fully: it is currently unlawful to recruit people for jobs based on personal characteristics such as gender or ethnicity except in circumstances where it can be proved that there is a genuine occupational requirement – for example where for a doctor to deal properly with predominantly female patients whose religion or faith require them not to be medically examined by a male doctor. In other words, the need for a job candidate to possess a particular personal characteristic has to be related to job requirements that are essential for satisfactory performance.

This is because the conventional view about equal opportunities is that it is unfair to select for jobs on the basis of personal characteristics such as gender, even when a job candidate possesses all the other job requirements. Merit must be the key factor in selecting people for jobs and merit has not, so far – except in circumstances where there is a genuine occupational requirement for the job as described above, been seen to include personal characteristics such as gender, and so on.

But this stance runs counter to the business case arguments for building diverse workforces: better delivery to diverse customer needs and preferences and more inclusive societies and the value that diversity can deliver in terms of ideas, perspectives, creativity and innovation. And, when law aims to drive greater diversity and inclusivity it is illogical to include dubious barriers which are counterproductive to progress.

Certain forms of individual differences such as educational qualifications, personal experience, skills, competences and work performance have been traditionally considered as legitimate criteria for assessing a person's suitability and merit for employment and career progression, while other forms of difference such as gender and ethnic origin have been considered inappropriate and irrelevant.

New ways of thinking are urgently needed about what personal forms of individual differences, abilities and traits, constitute 'merit' because 'merit' is rightly the cornerstone of fairness regarding equality, diversity and inclusion. This will enable good practice in diversity management to be refreshed and give more confidence to those making decisions about employment and training and more scope to trigger faster change in overturning the tables on outdated and misguided interpretations that currently inform good practice.

In fact, developments in thinking about diversity management are beginning to turn the tables on this and suggest that, rather than being considered irrelevant, personal characteristics such as gender and ethnicity and so on, should be taken into account.

Literature reviews show that diversity management scholars argue that individual differences are essential ingredients for high performance, creativity, innovation and competitive advantage. They explain that there are legal, moral, business, social and economic case arguments which illustrate that while diversity may contribute to business performance, ignoring it would have high-cost consequences for organisations and that the perception that diversity management is singularly a cost burden, is unfounded.

Such scholars see tensions between the current legal framework for diversity and the business case drivers which are often polar opposites that need to be reconciled to facilitate diversity progress.

In our view, the evidence shows that the business and legal case arguments for diversity management can and should be reconciled.

Some diversity scholars have argued that the main reason why diversity management has been adopted is its potential to add value to business performance and indeed the various CIPD research evidence about diversity and the business case show that it is the business case that drives interest beyond mere legal compliance and makes the difference between the leading-edge players in the field of equality, diversity and inclusion.

According to Cassell and Biswas (2000), the shift from equal opportunities to diversity management was triggered by individualised and performance-driven business case arguments. These marked a move away from the focus on emotive and moral case arguments associated with equal opportunities and the removal of unfair discrimination and has given diversity management and equal opportunities distinguishing characteristics based on the business case and legal,moral or social cases. However, we would argue that diversity management embraces legal,moral and social case arguments as part of the overarching business case.

There is of course cynicism about the business case for diversity. This has been fuelled by the increasing number of diversity issues that are surfacing for attention and the fact that there are many different definitions of diversity in use. '*Diversity means many things to many people*' is now a common caveat that precedes discussions on the topic.

> '*"Diversity means many things to many people"* is now a common caveat that precedes discussions on the topic.'

The existence of multiple definitions is cited as a stumbling block for diversity progress and the credibility of the business case that arguably inhibits uniform diversity progress. Descriptions of diversity are crowded with forms of difference which many organisations have yet to acknowledge or include in their diversity policies and practices. This is shown in the CIPD's state of the nation survey reports on diversity management.

In our view it is the failure to take into account the inclusive nature of diversity to enhance the benefits of difference that serves to undermine the business case for diversity, not the inclusive nature of diversity itself.

As defined and promoted by the CIPD, diversity management is about '*valuing everyone as an individual – valuing people as employees, customers and clients*'.

> '...diversity management is about *"valuing everyone as an individual – valuing people as employees, customers and clients"*.'

DIVERSITY MANAGEMENT AND BUSINESS PERFORMANCE

Diversity management literature suggests there are strong organisational reasons for adopting diversity management and the associated philosophy and approaches. In fact, the empirical evidence of a positive correlation between effective diversity management and improved organisational performance has been overwhelming in recent years.

For example, Barkema, Baum and Mannix (2002) position diversity as one of the main challenges facing management in the 21st century, and highlight evidence about a clear link between positive organisational outcomes and effective diversity management. Additionally, they refer to studies that examine the negative outcomes of diversity, and argue that the effective management of diversity delivers positive results and eliminates potential negative repercussions such as conflict in teams.

Recent international research from the Boston Consultancy Group shows that diversity is one of the top global issues for management attention (see box opposite).

Top five future challenges for companies in Europe

1   managing talent

2   managing demographics

3   becoming a learning organisation

4   managing work–life balance

5   managing change and cultural transformation

Source: Boston Consulting Group 2007

Our literature review shows there is growing evidence about the business benefits of diversity management at this level, too.

Raatikainen (2002) reviews case study evidence in support of the interplay between diversity management and business performance, showing a number of advantages, including improved creativity and customer focus through competitive practice of multiculturalism in the workplace.

Complementing this, Ozbilgin and Tatli (2008) argue that managing diversity in the headquarters of the global firm, is an important strategy through which global companies can gain strategic advantages from using their diverse local competencies in coordinating international operations.

GOING UP A GEAR WITH DIVERSITY MANAGEMENT TO MAKE MORE OF A DIFFERENCE TO PERFORMANCE

As we have noted earlier in this report, diversity has the potential to deliver both negative and positive impacts in organisations and, unless diversity is managed well the potential benefits will be missed. Controversially, this adds weight to the argument for the business case for diversity management rather than the legal, moral and social cases for simply becoming more diverse.

But managing diversity in organisations is in its infancy and an overview of various academic studies presents a complex picture of the challenges we face in aiming to pinpoint what good practice needs to address in the future to make sure we make the most of the increasingly diverse nature of the talent organisations need to sustain economic viability.

As we take the diversity and inclusion specialism up a gear to add value to performance we will need to move beyond the introduction of workplace policies and practices that focus on recruiting, rewarding and retaining diverse talent and responding smartly, effectively and efficiently to diverse customers and global customers. The responses we know are

imperative to make progress such as more flexibility, work–life balance, removal of unfair discrimination and bias, stamping out intimidating behaviour, bullying and harassment and the creation of open and harmonious workplace cultures will not be enough.

We will be searching for new management techniques and interventions that help us to enable people to work better together because of their diversity and not in spite of it. That is why insights we can gain from academic research will give us important clues about what to do next and why we are suggesting greater practitioner–academic collaboration through action research.

In brief, this chapter sets out some of the findings from a range of academic studies researched in the literature review carried out as part of our study of the business case for managing diversity.

Current research shows that different types of diversity have different impacts on performance and that time has a moderating effect.

Govindarajan and Gupta (2001) suggest there is an optimum level of diversity in teams and that the difference between cognitive and behavioural diversity should be taken into account.

They point out that while cognitive diversity is about the substantive differences in how individual members perceive the challenges facing teams and the behavioural diversity is about differences in language and culture. In their view cognitive diversity injects strength into teams, while behavioural diversity creates challenges that are a necessary evil to be minimised by careful management to reduce negative impacts on outcomes. Unfortunately, their study does not show how cultural differences stemming personal identity differences can be recognised and valued.

Research shows that time has an important impact on diversity management and outcomes and this influences the business case. While the negative effects of diversity may be short-term they are capable of being transformed into organisational benefits in the long term.

Watson, Kumar and Michaelsan (1993) illustrated this in their examination of the impact of diversity on interaction process and performance. Their research showed that although homogeneous teams performed better in the short term, heterogeneous (diverse) teams started performing much better after 17 weeks. This research highlights the way time influences diverse team behaviours and the importance of allowing time for diverse teams to learn how to work together in ways that can deliver added value to performance through their potential to be more creative than homogeneous teams. Homogeneity reinforces 'groupthink' which is directly counterproductive in terms of innovation, creativity, flexibility and team effectiveness.

Looking at two different ways of managing diversity – one from an inclusive approach and one from an exclusive group identity approach, Svyantek *et al* (2002) discovered that time influenced both. Inclusive approaches based on merit delivered better performance in the longer term. This supports our view that the inclusive nature of diversity beyond the exclusive issues protected in law on a group identity basis does not weaken the business case for diversity as long as such additional diversity issues are taken into account and integrated into the way organisations behave and develop their working processes and systems as well as their policies.

Larkey (1996) highlighted *categorisation* and *specification* as two processes that inform the way people stereotype each other and anticipate certain types of behaviours and how these expected behaviours are changed as a result of meeting and interacting with each other. So, the categories of gender and ethnicity for example may raise a person's expectations about the way a woman or an Italian might behave before they have met them. However, after meeting them the process of specification takes place as they get to know the person and make different observations about them on a piecemeal basis depending on what they talk about and how they actually behave. The difference between these two processes is that the categorisation process is based on preconceptions and misguided assumptions associated with the stereotype or assigned group identity. The research conclusion is that it is only when people meet and interact with each other that there is a reality check, albeit on a piecemeal basis, about the nature of diversity and that it is the specialisation process that has the greater potential to foster a more positive attitude to recognising diversity.

Taking diversity beyond the issues covered by law, a study of the value of knowledge-sharing and structural diversity by Cummings (2004) involving 182 work groups in the list of Fortune 500 companies reveals that the organisational value of knowledge-sharing increases if the work groups are structurally diverse, and the members have different affiliations, roles and positions.

> '...the organisational value of knowledge-sharing increases if the work groups are structurally diverse, and the members have different affiliations, roles and positions.'

In their study of the international construction industry, Dadfar and Gustavsson (1992) argue that, while there was evidence that cultural diversity delivered an advantage in management level project teams, there was no evidence of advantage at the workgroup level. However, when homogeneous cultural teams were put in competition with one another, the bonding influence of national pride meant they *did* deliver performance advantage. They also found that people with bicultural backgrounds were useful moderators in multicultural groups.

Despite the evidence that diversity can jeopardise workplace harmony and interactive processes, in a review of empirical evidence in literature, Hopkins and Hopkins (2002) reveal that cultural recomposition – the process by which the homogeneity of a team alters through the integration of new, culturally different, members – can be effectively managed without damaging the processes of team interactions if the professional attributes of the new member are emphasised, rather than social differences. This is a significant finding that may help to counter the initial potential difficulties found in work reported earlier in this document, suggesting that team heterogeneity may be characterised by problems with team harmony and employment relations in the initial stages.

Hopkins and Hopkins found that culture change can be effected in ways that deliver positive outcomes and, Mannix (2003) points to studies that show the relationships between different types of diversity and conflict, explaining that further research is crucial to find out how to use conflict associated with diversity in positive ways and tackle negative conflict and that exploring diversity and conflict in multiple forms will be more productive then seeking tenuous links between diversity strands and conflict.

Even though, as we have noted earlier, the evidence for the business case for diversity management remains patchy, nevertheless there is growing recognition that effective management of diversity can certainly generate performance improvements, both in the short and long term and in teams and organisations.

Beside the above specific studies, a large body of literature (see Ozbilgin and Tatli, 2008 for a comprehesive review) has also identified a further wide range of benefits from diversity management including:

❖ reducing the potential for backlash impact as associated with affirmative action

❖ meeting diverse customer demands more effectively

❖ improving understanding and ability to succeed in the complex globalisation of markets

❖ delivery of the *psychological contract*, improved employee relations and reduced labour turnover

❖ improvements in the quality and performance of internal workforce in terms of skills, creativity, problem solving and flexibility.

SOCIAL, ORGANISATIONAL AND PROFESSIONAL ASPECTS OF THE BUSINESS CASE FOR DIVERSITY

The current literature on the business case for managing diversity is well developed, but suffers from an exclusive focus on organisational issues.

Unfortunately this misses the value it adds to performance in macro, social and political contexts. In a complex socio-political context, it is a mistake solely to focus on diversity issues at the micro/organisational level because this fails to take account of the way diversity impacts in these wider areas and undermines comprehensive understanding of the business case arguments.

We also notice from our literature research that there is a gap in the focus on the organisational level business case for managing diversity. This misses consideration of a secondary analysis of the links between resources, processes, personal relationships, power and influence and performance outcomes.

We also suggest there is a need for a further level of analysis related to the impact that diversity professionals can deliver on successful diversity management.

Diversity professionals are key change agents in organisations regarding diversity progress, but the literature review we have carried out does not highlight the impact they can have.

In our research on diversity and the business case we have taken this into account in a multi-level approach to explore diversity management as:

❖ a negotiated prescription across a wide range of actors in the diversity industry of the contemporary social-political context of Britain

❖ a management approach that promotes difference in order to improve performance

❖ a process in which diversity professionals act as agents of change and seek to mobilise organisational resources in order to realise performance improvements through diversity management.

The next chapter uses this three-pronged framework in order to expose the state of the nation in the UK regarding the business case for diversity management.

THE BUSINESS CASE FOR DIVERSITY – 3
HOW PREVALENT IS IT IN PRACTICE?

❖ **While evidencing the business case for managing diversity we also wanted to find out how well it is understood and what significance it has in influencing organisations.**

❖ **In the next two chapters we draw from a range of field studies we carried out and a unique national level diversity survey undertaken by the Chartered Institute of Personnel and Development.**

WHAT WE FOUND

Our research shows that there is a wide range of understanding about the business case for diversity and what it comprises, and various views about its status and importance in influencing progress. Taking into account the views expressed by academics, government agencies, professional bodies, trade unions, trainers, diversity experts, specialists and consultants as well as professional bodies, it is clear that while there are keen advocates on the one hand, others depend on legal and moral case arguments which they see as separate from the business case rather than part of it.

WHAT WE THINK

Aspects of the business case:

❖ customer care and marketplace competitiveness

❖ corporate image, brand, ethics and values

❖ recruitment and retention of talent

❖ designing and delivering products and services

❖ increasing creativity and innovation

❖ being an employer of choice through effective people management and development

❖ complying with legislation

❖ corporate social responsibility

Source: Managing diversity: people make the difference at work but everyone is different (CIPD, 2005)

In our view, separating legal obligations and behaving morally from the business case is pedantic nonsense. Making sure legal duties are upheld and behaving ethically have serious cost implications if things go wrong – avoiding legal costs, ethical business behaviour and protecting corporate reputation are serious bottom line issues – and we would therefore include them as aspects of the generic business case.

Table 1 on page 10 sets out the key drivers for diversity in terms of business benefits.

WHAT THIS MEANS

Getting this message across will be vital to speeding up diversity progress as the evidence detailed later in this chapter shows. Overall, the understanding of the business case is still weak and it therefore punches below its true weight in effecting progress. This calls for considerable effort in education and awareness-raising about the inclusive nature of the business case and the development of tools and guidance to inform and influence good practice and organisational behaviour.

Table 1 ❖ **Key drivers for diversity in terms of business benefits (respondents ranked their top five on a scale of 1–5, with 1 being the most important)**

Drivers	Percentage of respondents					Overall importance
	Most important	Very important	Important	Less important	Least important	
To recruit and retain best talent	13	17	19	8	7	**64**
Because it makes business sense	17	14	14	7	8	**60**
To improve business performance	6	10	15	10	7	**48**
To address recruitment problems	8	11	12	8	7	**46**
Desire to improve customer relations	5	8	15	8	7	**43**
To improve products and services	10	9	13	5	7	**44**
To improve creativity and innovation	6	8	14	8	7	**43**
Desire to reach diverse markets	6	7	11	7	8	**39**
To improve corporate branding	5	7	13	7	5	**37**
To enhance decision-making	3	8	15	5	4	**35**
To respond to the competition in the market	6	6	10	7	4	**33**
To respond to the global market	6	3	8	6	7	**30**

Source: Diversity in business: a focus for progress. (CIPD, 2007)

WHAT WE FOUND

From the interviews we carried out, even though there is wide reference to the business case for diversity – which is good news – the rhetoric we heard was not supported by significant relevant action customised to benefit individual organisations. Rather, organisational responses appear to mimic the predominant approach adopted in the particular economic sector.

WHAT THIS SUGGESTS

To enable organisations to move forward using the business case they need to understand and be able to contextualise the generic arguments, in order to make sure that the actions taken support the delivery of organisational objectives, visions and values.

This suggests that to help people with responsibility for diversity to be more effective in what they do they need to have:

❖ an appreciation of the national level diversity scene and what drives change

❖ familiarity with the different national level stakeholder interests regarding diversity management

❖ up-to-date knowledge of the way thinking about diversity management is evolving

❖ access to networks to share knowledge and understanding and to increase personal learning

❖ communication and influencing skills and a willingness to share knowledge and experience about both the internal and external diversity scenes

❖ a sophisticated appreciation of the diversity business case and how to use it appropriately to influence change in the way organisations do things.

THE BUSINESS CASE NEEDS MORE SUPPORT

'It is clear from research that the business case for diversity management is an important driver for change yet there is huge potential for it to make a bigger difference than our research evidence shows it currently does.

> '...the business case for diversity management is an important driver for change yet there is huge potential for it to make a bigger difference...'

To support this statement we draw on the unique national level survey carried out by the Chartered Institute of Personnel and Development to explore the state of the nation on diversity management and the influence of the business case for diversity at organisational level.

This survey has generated 285 completed electronic questionnaires by people responsible for diversity management in organisations across the UK. The sample included a representation of organisations by size, region and economic sector. Twenty-one per cent of respondents were female. The median age of respondents was between 41 and 50 and most were in middle and senior management posts with unit- or organisation-wide responsibility for diversity.

WHAT ARE THE ORGANISATIONAL DRIVERS FOR MANAGING DIVERSITY?

Some academics argue that diversity management and equal opportunities are driven by different external and internal pressures.

While diversity progress is seen to be driven by voluntary responses related to internal business case arguments and everyday business realities the pressure for equal opportunities progress is seen to be compliant with the external pressures imposed by regulation (McDougall, 1996, Thomas, 1990).

This influences two prevailing assumptions about the drivers for diversity management

❖ diversity management is driven by business case arguments

❖ diversity management is not driven by legal enforcement

But while the literature on diversity management suggests that progress is dependent on business case arguments rather than law, the CIPD survey shows that legal compliance pips the business case arguments to the post in having a major influence. Diversity management is significantly influenced by law.

> 'Diversity management is significantly influenced by law.'

Table 2 ❖ Top-ranking drivers for managing diversity	Percentage of respondents citing as 'most important'
Legal pressures	32
Because it makes business sense	17
To be an employer of choice	15
To recruit and retain best talent	13
Because it is morally right	13
Corporate social responsibility	13
To improve products and services	10
Belief in social justice	9
To address recruitment problems	8
Desire to reach diverse markets	6
To improve business performance	6
To respond to the global market	6
To respond to the competition in the market	6
To improve creativity and innovation	6
Desire to improve customer relations	5
To improve corporate branding	5
To enhance decision-making	3
Trade union activities	3

Source: Diversity in business: how much progress have employers made? First findings. (CIPD, 2007)

The CIPD survey results show that the most important motivation for managing diversity is 'legal pressures', with 68% of the respondents ranking it among the top five drivers included in the survey. These were 'to recruit and retain best talent' (64%), 'corporate social responsibility' (62%), 'to be an employer of choice' (62%), and 'because it makes business sense' (60%).

Nevertheless, the survey shows the business case for diversity is important, too, with the main arguments relating to the recruitment and retention of talent. This aspect of the business case is primarily a human resource management driver and while it is very important, this predominant but narrow focus exposes the way in which organisations are failing to grasp the wider aspects of the business case and the way in which managing diversity can deliver further benefits to business performance.

The CIPD survey findings show how the concept of managing diversity as a guiding business principle is not integrated into the logic of other business functions such as marketing, product development and customer relations. Not enough organisations are making the connections between the impact of demographics and the supply of talent and those which influence the markets for products and services even though the importance of recognising diversity in the marketplace to improve business performance is recognised. This lack of 'joined-up' thinking is letting business performance down.

> **'Not enough organisations are making the connections between the impact of demographics and the supply of talent...'**

Based on our research findings we maintain that that the rhetorical polarisation of the drivers for managing diversity between legal compliance and specific bottom-line business issues is not only unhelpful but is also artificial, inappropriate and an unnecessary distraction. In fact, rather than trying to argue the supremacy of any one individual driver for managing diversity it makes more sense to embrace a diversity of reasons as components of the business case. This case for diversity management is strengthened by including:

❖ a wider range of diversity management drivers

❖ business, legal, moral case and social responsibility arguments

❖ a wide range of organisational stakeholder interests and benefits related to progressing diversity management.

THE BUSINESS CASE FOR DIVERSITY – 4
HOW MUCH DIFFERENCE IS IT MAKING?

❖ **Do employers measure the impact of what they do?**

❖ **Leading-edge organisations in diversity management have been encouraged to take into account a broader range of personal characteristics which can cause unfair disadvantage. This development has been influenced by the extension of legal protection in the UK to meet EU requirements on discrimination. For example age, sexual orientation, religion and belief and the growing interest in and increasing knowledge about diversity and inclusion.**

The focus on managing diversity has attracted cynical responses from exponents of equal opportunities who argue that the explosion of diversity issues will result in less attention on equality rather than more. However, this criticism is not substantiated by our examination of organisational policies and practices.

Evidence from the CIPD national level diversity survey shows the extent to which employers take into account a broad range of diversity issues – including diversity issues that are not covered by discrimination law.

As can be seen from Table 3 on page 14, a wide range of diversity issues are covered by organisational policies. Issues with legal protection are cited more frequently than those which are not and are given fairly similar attention although, strikingly, disability is mentioned the most often.

We know that having written policies is not enough to drive diversity progress into mainstream activities, so the CIPD diversity survey asked respondents to say how they make sure their diversity policies are taken into account in organisational practices.

Awareness raising and diversity training for employees comes top, being mentioned by 65.6 % of respondents. Employee attitude surveys (61.8 %) are the second most common activity. But responses showed only a small minority of organisations undertake activities that would make diversity management systemic. For example, diversity is a performance criterion in only 18.6 % of the organisations covered by the survey and only 15.8% include diversity-related goals in managers' performance assessments. Furthermore, 95.1% of the organisations represented in the survey do not reward or recognise diversity achievements, 70.5% do not build diversity objectives into business goals and only 20% use diversity standards, while 69.8 % do not set diversity objectives.

From the range of activities reported in the CIPD survey it appears that diversity management in UK organisations is generally superficial. This points to the need for:

❖ greater understanding of the external and internal drivers that make diversity management an essential business process

❖ better implementation to move policy aspirations into practice

❖ wider adoption of customised business case arguments

❖ the inclusion of diversity objectives into performance management systems

❖ the wider adoption of monitoring and evaluation processes.

A diversity sophistication index was developed from the CIPD survey results and organisations can make a broad reference to this to see how well they are doing themselves.

The index incorporates 146 variables based on macro-level and organisational-level drivers and organisational-level diversity policies and practices. The most sophisticated organisation represented in the survey scored 122 marks out of a highest possible score of 146 while the lowest score of zero was achieved by five organisations. The average sophistication score was 52.

As can be seen in Table 4 on page 14, there is considerable variation across organisations in terms of levels of sophistication. The differences relate to organisational size and economic sector. Large organisations and public sector organisations have higher scores than smaller organisations in

Table 3 ❖ Diversity issues taken into account by employers	
	Number of respondents
Accent	7
Postcode	8
Weight	9
Political ideology	27
Physical appearance	31
Mental health	39
Social and economic background	47
All forms of difference	57
Trade union membership	61
Criminal convictions	61
Parental status	87
Marital status	120
Age	130
Nationality	138
Sexual orientation	159
Religion	160
Gender/sex	165
Ethnicity/race	166
Disability	170

Table 4 ❖ Business case and legal case cross-tabulation (in percentages)				
		Legal case		
		No	Yes	Total
Business case	No	20	20	40
	Yes	11	49	60
Total		31	69	100

Base: 277 respondents

Source: Diversity in business: a focus for progress. (CIPD, 2007)

the private and voluntary sectors. Table 4 illustrates the frequencies of sophistication scores.

The diversity sophistication index points to the need for:

❖ more information and guidance about how to make a customised business case to bring about diversity progress, taking into account contextualised circumstances

❖ organisations to look beyond custom and practice in the same economic sector to inform what they do, as the level of sophistication in diversity management generally appears to be low

❖ organisations to draw on a wider range of good practice guidance and case study material to be more successful in managing diversity, taking advantage of sources such as networks, conferences, training and education opportunities and web-based information for examples of good practice.

DO EMPLOYERS STRIVE TO SHOW THE IMPACT OF MANAGING DIVERSITY ON BUSINESS PERFORMANCE?

To be successful in influencing diversity progress, organisations need to be able to show that what they do makes a difference and adds real value. But the CIPD survey suggests that organisations generally need to be much smarter at doing this than they appear to be.

While they use indicators and measures of change such as employee attitude surveys, complaint and grievance and labour turnover statistics, tools such as a balanced score card and impact assessments, which can show the links between diversity management and customer satisfaction and business performance are used less frequently (see Table 5, opposite).

Based on the CIPD survey findings, it is clear that there needs to be a greater focus on evaluating approaches to managing diversity and much more attention needs to be paid to:

❖ the wider use of key diversity performance indicators

❖ balanced scorecards mainstreaming diversity objectives into business goals and objectives, related to product development and service delivery targets, for example.

For more detailed information about the CIPD diversity survey results see *Diversity in business: how much progress have employers made?* (2006) and *Diversity in business: a focus for progress.* (2007).

Table 5 ❖ Which of the following measures do (or would) you use to monitor diversity in your organisation?	
Measures	**Count**
Employee attitude surveys	206
Number of complaints and grievances	161
Labour turnover	159
Employee perfomance appraisals	132
Absenteeism	129
Ability to recruit	114
Number of tribunal cases	89
Impact assessment	77
Level of customer satisfaction	67
Employee commitment surveys	55
Business performance	53
Balanced scorecard	48
Diversification of customer base	37
Improvements to problem-solving and decision-making	19
Psychological contract issues	16

THE BUSINESS CASE FOR DIVERSITY – HOW MUCH DIFFERENCE IS IT MAKING?

15

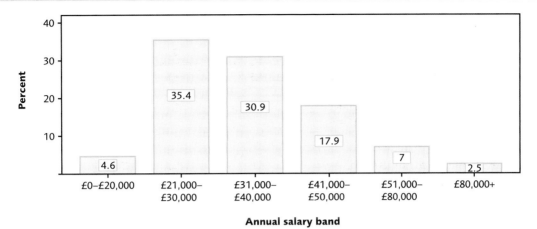

Figure 1 ❖ **Annual salaries of respondents working in diversity management**

Based on the CIPD survey findings it is clear that diversity progress could be speeded up by :

❖ promoting the business case arguments for managing diversity and the inclusive nature of the business case

❖ helping people to contextualise business case arguments and be confident in doing this

❖ addressing ways of helping those given responsibility for progressing diversity to acquire the knowledge, expertise and relationship management, negotiating and influencing skills to do this well, so that progressing diversity becomes a mainstream business issue and part of everyone's job

❖ positioning the change agents given responsibility for progressing the diversity agenda at appropriate levels in an organisation to give them the necessary authority and gravitas

❖ gaining and communicating senior management support for diversity progress

❖ allocating budgets to help drive change

❖ giving those with responsibility for diversity access to appropriate formal training and skills development opportunities

❖ encouraging participation in facilitated external diversity networking to keep up to date with good practice in diversity management and practical learning.

MANAGING DIVERSITY BETTER – MAKING MORE OF WHAT WE KNOW

6

❖ **Linking theory and practice to make more of what we already know about managing diversity makes sense. Since the concept evolved in the mid-1990s much has been learned and observed by practitioners and academics. Yet, so far we have failed to pool this expertise in a working relationship to deliver exponential learning and enhanced knowledge which can then be shared with wider audiences, using a well-designed communication strategy. This is a national-level challenge for public policy-makers.**

In this chapter we argue that closer academic–practitioner collaboration could make a significant difference. Based on our own experiences of running an action research programme on managing diversity, we explain how this can be done. First we turn to the literature on academic–practitioner collaboration to show why we think going down this avenue is enticing.

ACADEMIC–PRACTITIONER COLLABORATION: THE WAY FORWARD

A schism between academic- versus practitioner-orientated research is noted by Tranfield and Starkey (1998). Management researchers promote their own approaches to knowledge creation and transfer. Some focus on the development of theoretical knowledge and the identification of generic principles which can be universally applied regardless of contextual circumstances (for example, Hitt, 1998). Others focus on identifying applied knowledge and the adoption of variables that easily relate to organisational goals (Thomas and Tymon, 1982).

WHAT IS THE RESEARCH/PRACTICE GAP?

The research/practice gap is rooted in the different frames of reference and basic assumptions academics and practitioners make about such things as the types of information believed to constitute valid bases for action, the ways in which information is analysed and categorised, the past experience used to evaluate the validity of knowledge claims, and the metaphors used to symbolically construct the world in meaningful ways. So we ask, how can we 'mind the gap'?

The role of learning

Our response is rooted in shared learning. Learning is conceptualised as a virtuous circle in which new information is used to challenge existing ideas in order to develop new perspectives and understanding and better ways of doing things.

What we need to engineer is academic–practitioner dialogue to speed up the learning that is needed to inform more quickly the responses we need to make to take advantage of the opportunities offered by diversity and overcome the negative consequences of ignoring it. In our view, better collaboration between academics and practitioners will arm practitioners with the knowledge they need to address the challenges and opportunities more effectively and efficiently if the implications of this knowledge are made explicit in practical terms.

> '...better collaboration between academics and practitioners will arm practitioners with the knowledge they need to address the challenges and opportunities more effectively...'

A VISION FOR THE FUTURE

In our view, working together is an essential way forward to expedite the evolution of good practice in managing diversity. For this reason we recommend the way forward is facilitated networking rooted in solution-focused problem-solving, and we set out our thoughts and experiences below.

Setting the scene for learning

Learning involves the transfer of knowledge among different communities – mainly through inter-community cooperation and collaboration – that stimulates the creation of new knowledge and contributes to the ability of communities to innovate and change. At the same time, inter-disciplinary learning needs people with different expertise to be prepared to challenge the tenets of their own disciplines. Paradoxically, the very disciplines they are schooled in can be both a barrier to knowledge transfer and learning as well as a bridge. People who have different perspectives will seek to defend these in the face of challenges to preserve the validity of what they know and their personal comfort with their frames of reference. The process of letting go and moving on takes convincing evidence and personal confidence, but these defensive processes are also the fuel for driving common understanding.

Knowledge transfer and learning takes place best in a shared context based on cooperation and trust. This helps multi-disciplinary communities to modify their knowledge and understanding, gain critical competencies and challenge their collective definitions of their organisational and professional identities.

So how can a collaborative knowledge-sharing and learning about managing diversity be fostered? We set out our ideas below.

Knowledge creation about managing diversity through collaboration

Diversity practitioners do not exist in isolation. They operate in macro-structural, meso-organisational and micro-relational contexts. Their multi-level engagement with different sets of stakeholders makes it possible for them to benefit from knowledge creation through collaboration.

> **Diversity practitioners do not exist in isolation. They operate in macro-structural, meso-organisational and micro-relational contexts.**

In Nonaka and Takeuchi's (1995) model and other similar models (for example, Choo, 1998; Leonard-Barton, 1995), new knowledge is seen as being created most rapidly when there is continual conversion from tacit to explicit and from explicit to tacit knowledge. According to Nonaka and colleagues, knowledge creation increases through four interactive methods of knowledge conversion: socialisation (tacit to tacit), externalisation (tacit to explicit), combination (explicit to explicit) and internationalisation (explicit to tacit).

Nonaka and Takeuchi suggest that unless successful socialisation occurs between academics and practitioners – with each side truly understanding and empathising with each other – attempts to transfer explicit knowledge across boundaries are likely to fail. In the absence of effective intergroup socialisation, the independent social identities of academics and practitioners are likely to strengthen (Ashforth and Mael, 1991), with associated increases in in-group and out-group thinking reducing the motivation for each side to learn from the other (Weick, 1995). The current situation regarding diversity–scholar and diversity–practitioner collaboration mirrors this. Neither turns to the other routinely or in a structured way, even though there are rare examples of academic–practitioner partnering generating collaborative learning about managing diversity.

In socialisation, tacit knowledge is exchanged through joint activities, such as individuals spending time together or learning together, in order to produce some form of shared mental model, frame of reference, or culture that can then serve as a framework for moving forward. Because socialisation involves acceptance of the beliefs, feelings and emotions of others, it is very difficult to achieve without some form of shared face-to-face experience. In this sense, because knowledge transfer is fundamentally a social process, the power of increased interaction between academics and practitioners for generating new knowledge should not be underestimated, even when such interactions are not explicitly research-oriented.

> **'...the power of increased interaction between academics and practitioners for generating new knowledge should not be underestimated...'**

Tacit knowledge is transferred from person to person by being 'externalised'. For example, 'know-how' needs to be made explicit in ways that make it accessible by someone else, possibly by being written down, so that it can be absorbed or 'internalised'. During the process of internalisation, explicit knowledge is converted to tacit knowledge through learning by doing.

Action research is a process based on learning by doing which can be used to help transfer explicit academic and practical knowledge about managing diversity between academics and diversity practitioners, and to develop new shared knowledge which can influence both academic theories and good practice.

> **'Most published academic research relating to managing diversity fails to take account of practitioner perspectives.'**

Most published academic research relating to managing diversity fails to take account of practitioner perspectives. It combines explicit knowledge from different academic disciplines and produces new syntheses about how to do things by translating academic findings into practitioner language.

Published academic research which fails to take into account the practical aspects of managing diversity is not likely to respond to the needs of practitioners. Furthermore, it requires readers to be sufficiently well-informed to be able to evaluate the findings rigorously and objectively, the research methods used to explore the issues identified for investigation and to judge what practical application they might have.

Additionally, practitioners may find it difficult to face up to results that expose indications of poor practice. This could raise concerns about how to implement any desirable change – especially where a practitioner has little influence or power. Such de-motivating experiences do not generally serve to build interest in academic material.

For academic–practitioner collaboration to be successful in supporting organisational change it is important to take into account the demoralising effects of 'fear of failure'.

It is difficult to pre-judge the level of practitioner appetite to implement research findings. Personal, cultural and organisational factors will influence this. In any case, the implementation of evidence-based research findings is associated with two closely linked problems. The first involves decisions about the value of the findings and the second is how to implement them if they are valuable.

Those who publish research seem to take it for granted that practitioners will fall over themselves to adopt the findings and

act on them. Nothing could be further from the truth and, until the stakeholder interests of practitioners are taken into account in the way research is carried out, the efforts made by academics will remain just that – academic. We need new ways to enable research to be put into practice so we can reinforce the worth they have by tracking what difference they make and sharing this learning. Such an approach will provide a powerful way of progressing diversity management in ways that add value for all stakeholders.

Table 10 below shows how the features of professional and academic knowledge are polarised and contribute to the challenges for academic–practitioner collaboration on managing diversity.

It does not make sense to ignore the knowledge gap between academic research findings related to diversity and the practice of diversity management. Addressing it could help to create new knowledge about diversity management much more quickly and bring benefit to all stakeholders.

In the next chapter we explain how we carried out a diversity action research programme to bring together the knowledge of academics and practitioners regarding the business case for diversity and create new understanding about issues relating to driving progress.

Table 10 ❖ Features of professional and academic knowledge on managing diversity	
Features of professional knowledge and practices	Features of academic knowledge and practices
Social	Impersonal
Tacit (based on training and experience)	Explicit (systematic/supported)
Situational: ability to understand a specific context	Universal: ability to look for global characteristics
Credibility is judged by good actions, how well you manage people and produce reports	Credibility is judged by written discourses, research output and teaching responsibilities
'Just-in-time' practice, expedient decision-making	Considered and thoughtful decisions
Ability to make judgements	Ability to discuss and debate ideas
Local knowledge valued over scholarly and academic knowledge	Scholarly and global knowledge valued over local knowledge
Concern with relevance	Concern with rigour

Source: *Intersecting worlds: inherent tensions and new practices in doctoral study.* (Jane Malfroy, 2002). Fourth International Biennial Conference on Professional Doctorates.

THE BUSINESS CASE FOR DIVERSITY – WHAT ACTION RESEARCH SHOWS US

7

❖ **How we designed and managed an action learning research programme to explore the business case for managing diversity and how it can add value to business performance.**

❖ **The issues that surfaced from this process which face the people responsible for diversity.**

As part of the CIPD's agenda to research the business case for managing diversity in 2002, Dianah Worman, the CIPD's Adviser for diversity commissioned Drs Gary Mulholland and Mustafa Ozbilgin, academics specialising in business and marketing and employment relations, to lead a diversity action research programme to explore why and how organisations drive the diversity agenda, to support them in doing this and help them focus on business objectives to add value to business performance.

The action research is described in detail in two published CIPD reports. One is in the CIPD change agenda, *Managing diversity: learning by doing* (2005), and is available free from www.cipd.co.uk. The other, *Managing diversity: words into action* (2006), is an executive briefing available from the CIPD bookstore at www.cipd.co.uk/bookstore.

To run the CIPD diversity action research programme a diverse team of different specialists was set up. It included diversity specialists, human resource practitioners, business management consultants as well as academics with backgrounds in marketing, employment relations and diversity.

This team worked with people with different levels of understanding and experience in managing diversity, recruited from 12 diverse organisations – both large and small – from the public, private and voluntary sectors of the economy.

The action research programme set out to explore the business case for diversity in these different organisational contexts and inform the progress and shape of organisational diversity initiatives.

Targeted organisations were invited to an explanatory event designed to engage interest and commitment in taking part.

The event put people in the picture about the purpose of the action research, the benefits of taking part and what they would be expected to do. To protect sensitivities, encourage the free exchange of information and sustain engagement with the action research programme a protocol was agreed by all those taking part to ensure their full participation and personal contributions, as the success of the programme depended on this and people's personal responsibilities to each other.

An initial briefing session took place to introduce those taking part to a common set of ideas for diversity research topics and help them to decide what they could do to have an impact on a relevant business-related challenge in their own organisations.

This briefing session was designed to be informative about diversity, explanatory about the research and participative to trigger group discussion.

It included a summary of the findings of the literature review about the business case for diversity which the academics had carried out and the propositions they had put forward in a working paper which we refer to in more detail below. It also introduced the basic concepts of action research.

We found that action research, which is defined as:

> *...a participatory, democratic process concerned with developing practical knowing in the pursuit of worthwhile human purposes...'*

> Reason & Bradbury (2001)

is particularly appropriate for solving the complex issues surrounding diversity management.

This complexity runs deep, even to the extent of basic understanding about what managing diversity is about. At the beginning of the CIPD action research programme, which lasted for three years, we found it was necessary to discuss this in detail with participants so all those taking part had a common understanding and appreciated the legitimacy of different levels of sophistication regarding the management of diversity in different organisational contexts.

A working paper was drawn up by the academic team members to inform the action research programme and those taking part in it about managing diversity and the business case. This was based on the prevailing evidence for the business case taken from a literature review they carried out.

The working paper, examined eight main propositions taken from the literature review to show the interplay between managing diversity and business performance, and put forward the adoption of the balanced scorecard technique – a business management tool often used to guide and measure business objectives – as a mechanism for integrating good diversity practice into all operational activities.

The working paper was refined throughout the diversity action research programme, taking into account the field-study work carried out as part of the action research programme, the organisations taking part in it and additional anecdotal evidence drawn from a broader range of case studies.

The final published paper provides interesting insights into what links diversity with business performance and the techniques that can be used to integrate and mainstream diversity into operational activities. It is a CIPD Change Agenda called *Managing Diversity: linking theory and practice to business performance* (CIPD 2005) and is available free at www.cipd.co.uk in the research insight series of reports.

The action research field studies explored different aspects of the eight propositions developed in the working paper, the relevance they had to the way the organisations taking part operated and the diversity challenge they faced. The eight propositions consisted of:

❖ Diversity in employment promotes cost-effective employment relations

❖ Diversity enhances customer relations

❖ Diversity enhances creativity, flexibility and innovation in organisations

❖ Diversity promotes sustainable development and business advantage

❖ Diversity diminishes 'cultural relatedness'

❖ Flexibility, which diversity encourages, needs to be financially supported

❖ Diversity may jeopardise workplace harmony

❖ Organisational slack and tight fit may conflict.

Each organisation focused on one or more of them in their individual level research programmes and reflected on their relevance.

Those taking part in the action research had to take into account and reflect on academic theory, and draw insights from their own diversity practices in order to behave as reflexive practitioners.

Unsurprisingly, we discovered that diversity was a sensitive issue in most of the organisations taking part in the action research. Consequently, the individuals we worked with had to learn how to act as change agents and negotiate how to take forward what they wanted to do. This underlined the importance of personal influencing and change management skills.

It also became apparent that people needed to develop their research skills in order to carry out relevant research in their own organisations to inform their decisions and actions.

They were given guidance in doing this and a modified action research model was designed to inform and support the development of new knowledge and understanding about managing diversity and the effective exchange of ideas between both the academics and practitioners taking part (see Figure 2, opposite).

As well as the individual level guidance and mentoring that took place as part of the field work, there were regular group meetings. These helped people to learn from each other by reflecting on group discussions and what they were doing on a personal level. In this way, new knowledge and understanding were created for everyone based on both group and individual learning.

The group meetings helped people to get to know each other. This encouraged private meetings between group members who wanted to focus on things of particular concern to them in more detail. These private meetings in turn helped to inform both the group learning and individual activities.

The views and observations of fellow group members, the diversity specialists, academics and business consultants helped to shape and inform the development of personal-level research and organisational diversity initiatives, as well as the overarching research by the academics.

The iterative process that formed the basis of the action research built new knowledge for everyone taking part, because learning was shared about experiences, problems and concerns and achievements. People used the shared learning to reflect on their personal learning. This influenced what they did in their own organisations to progress diversity and, when this information was fed back to the group, it enhanced the group knowledge and understanding.

Figure 2 ❖ **Diversity action research model**

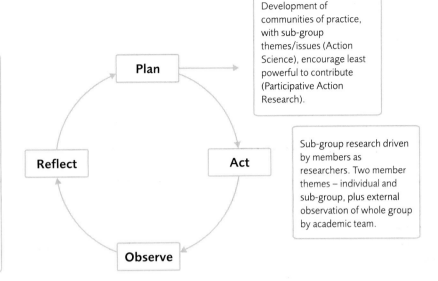

Action research model (Mulholland, Ozbilgin and Worman, 2005)

This action research programme helped the practitioners involved to revise their personal goals in driving diversity and to deliver better outcomes. It built levels of personal confidence and helped the academics to identify relevant material that might support and inform good diversity practice.

WHAT WE LEARNED ABOUT THE BUSINESS CASE FOR DIVERSITY FROM THE CIPD ACTION RESEARCH PROGRAMME

The CIPD executive briefing referred to earlier, *Managing diversity: words into action* (2006), details the initiatives carried out by those taking part in the action research programme, how they were carried out and what impact they had. This report also draws lessons and lists recommendations from the work we carried out.

In summary, the key findings from action research show that understanding about managing diversity is very varied and that there is a need to raise awareness. It is clear, however, that managing diversity does make business sense even in very different organisations, and that linking actions to business challenges and objectives ensures that what is done adds value to business performance.

The business case can be used in both large and small organisations and in those with sophisticated and less sophisticated approaches.

However, from the evidence we gained it is very important to make a business case for action relevant. This can be done by taking into account the particular contextual circumstances of

an organisation and showing how proposed actions will deliver benefits that will add value.

Predetermined performance measures or criteria – whether these are quantitative or qualitative – should be identified to show how success will be judged, communicated and celebrated.

A separate CIPD change agenda produced as part of the research carried out on the business case for managing diversity gives information about the importance of measurement and evaluation and discusses the use of the balanced scorecard which is often used in business as a mangement tool. *Managing diversity: measuring success* (2006) is available free at www.cipd.co.uk.

As well as strengthening and informing the business case arguments for diversity, the action research programme threw up other learning about the issues faced in driving progress. We refer to these below. Many add substance to the findings we mention earlier in Chapter 5.

KEY POINTS LEARNED

Key things we learned about the difficulties of driving diversity progress from those responsible for it and what they suggested are that different stakeholders have different fears and sensitivities and different levels of motivation regarding diversity issues. One organisation we worked with adopted the mantra 'reach out, value people, be courageous' to help people to speak out.

The action research highlighted the following as important to support diversity progress:

Change management skills and processes

❖ stakeholder management

❖ engagement and managing resistance

❖ maintaining momentum

❖ understanding cultural impacts.

Tactics

❖ helping people to feel involved in the training, rather than subjected to it

❖ engaging more people in diversity initiatives to help develop understanding

❖ involving trade union representatives in training and focus groups so they are engaged

❖ running focus groups to gain opinions and involvement

❖ organising fun events such as diversity competitions to encourage participation in order to increase knowledge and understanding

❖ using mixed focus groups to show how relevant diversity is; for example, including people from the human resource function in customer focus initiatives

❖ piggybacking on any other relevant initiatives

❖ recognising that line management motivation is key

❖ using 'quick wins' to help get buy-in

Getting top management on board

❖ senior management needs to be actively involved in initiatives to get more buy-in from everyone else – aim high and don't be satisfied with lip service

❖ check senior management is not just 'caught up' but 'signed up' and that they don't just find it easier to seek forgiveness than give support

❖ encourage senior managers to take a lead in not tolerating unacceptable behaviours such as bullying

❖ encourage top management to get tough with those lagging behind agreed actions to progress diversity

❖ get top management to understand that key individuals driving diversity need back-up support from senior colleagues

❖ be wary of hindsight in senior managers when faced with success or questions like 'Why weren't we doing this already?'

❖ don't be fooled by their acceptance of diversity as a principle – the going gets tougher when action is required

❖ make leaders aware of how important they are in personally supporting diversity openly and in being well informed

❖ help them to see that good leadership is needed to build the courage in others to deal with unacceptable behaviours

❖ top executives need to know they are key populations as change agents

❖ leaders should know they need to align customer and internal behaviours

❖ it requires imagination, even sneakiness, to get senior management on board.

Things go better in progressing diversity when people lead change

❖ balance emotional and business factors

❖ learn to manage individuals as well as groups

❖ act with patience – hand-holding and teaching where necessary

❖ try to correct ignorance and misunderstanding rather than being critical

❖ acknowledge how scary dealing with diversity is for many people

❖ explore individual views and change approaches accordingly

❖ share their knowledge

Good diversity communications are vital. To get messages across successfully:

❖ take into account workplace cultures

❖ it is more successful to use positive language and focus on diversity opportunities

❖ involving outsiders helps to spot meaningless organisational jargon

❖ note that impersonal communications don't engage people

❖ using interactive communication is more successful, especially for dealing with sensitive issues.

Measurement and evaluation observations

❖ view progress as distance covered – from the starting point to the goal rather than the goals achieved – this recognises effort, time and success

❖ increase the number of measures you use and don't rely on one set of criteria

❖ use the eyes and ears of those involved in diversity training or other initiatives to assess how the messages are transforming into new behaviours

❖ adopt hard measures to support the business case for diversity, such as the cost of harassment, employee retention rates, numbers of complaints, grievances and court cases

❖ carry out well-designed, properly targeted attitude surveys

❖ don't depend on out-of-date and inappropriate HR systems

❖ use indicators that are specific to an initiative.

Keep going and learn to cope with frustration caused by:

❖ perceptions of slow progress

❖ constantly reminding people of why managing diversity is important

❖ the time it takes for the business case to sink in

❖ the level of resistance encountered

❖ people who profess to have passion but don't take action.

Take heart from the satisfaction you can get from success

❖ 'I felt rewarded by the success of the diversity initiative and making a difference.'

❖ 'It is wonderful to see the results of my work.'

❖ 'It feels great to make a difference – however small.'

❖ 'It's empowering to feel you can make a difference.'

❖ 'It's a real privilege to see change happen, have a direct impact on others and be adding value to the bottom line of the organisation you work for.'

PEPPING UP THE PACE OF PROGRESS – SOME IDEAS
8

✤ **The evidence that diversity management contributes to business performance continues to grow. However, this message needs to be communicated better to raise the level of awareness and gain employer engagement.**

As we show in this report an inspection of the evidence using a variety of research methods points in the same direction – there *is* a business case but it is much broader in nature than it is often perceived to be. As we argue, the generic business case includes compliance with legal obligations, moral and social reasons, because all of these impact on the way organisations are run. It is, therefore, misleading and disingenuous to separate them because this becomes a distraction that gets in the way of diversity progress.

The evidence shows that organisations clearly need to understand better the inclusive nature of the generic business case. They also need to know how to contextualise this to trigger systemic change by taking into account specific organisational issues and circumstances to design diversity initiatives that can support business goals and add value.

The CIPD has published and promotes a range of information about managing diversity and the business case, much of which we have referred to and list in the References. In the main, this information is available free on the CIPD's website and an interactive business tool entitled *How to build your own business case for diversity and inclusion* has been developed to help CIPD members in formulating a customised business case [www.cipd.co.uk/subjects].

We have already pointed to the importance of raising awareness about the business case and we recommend that this should be a key objective for the new Equality and Human Rights Commission and a cornerstone of Government public policy interventions related to diversity progress.

We feel a national-level communication strategy would help to get organisations on board and, drawing on our experience of

facilitated networking which was the basis of the CIPD diversity action research programme, we recommend that ideally this should be accompanied by a facilitated networking opportunity accessible to those charged with driving this agenda in organisations. This facilitated networking in driving diversity progress should supplement, not replace, the activities of the many existing issue-specific diversity networks that focus on information sharing and benchmarking.

Drawing on the CIPD unique state-of-the-nation survey on diversity, it is clear that it is the business case that differentiates the leaders from the followers in diversity management, but that the comprehensive nature of the business case is not yet having the potential impact it could. This is why we feel a national-level awareness campaign could help to make a difference in closing the gap between the theory and scientific evidence related to the business benefits of diversity, which we identified from our review of the academic literature on the causal link between diversity management and performance improvements, and the practice of diversity management.

This gap fuels the difference between rhetoric and reality and could be reduced through academic–practitioner collaboration using the action research model we adopted for the CIPD diversity action research. The new knowledge gained from this collaboration could then be shared with all stakeholders interested in diversity progress as part of the national communication strategy we call for.

Because universities are required to contribute to their running costs in connection with the role they have to generate knowledge and develop skills, over the last three decades many have started to work closely with employers on a wide range of social topics including diversity management. But there is still huge potential for the nature of this collaboration to increase. For example, in connection with diversity management, much more use could be made of joint conferences, meetings and collaborative projects to share knowledge and develop mutual understanding. And, based on our experience, there is no doubt that action research has the potential to make a significant contribution to the growth of the knowledge we need to support the progress of managing diversity in practice.

REFERENCES

CIPD-PUBLISHED RESEARCH ON DIVERSITY

CIPD (2003)

Diversity: stacking up the evidence: a review of knowledge. Executive briefing. London: CIPD.

CIPD (2006)

Diversity in business: how much progress have employers made? First findings. Survey report. London: CIPD.

CIPD (2007)

Diversity in business: a focus for progress. Survey report. London: CIPD.

MULHOLLAND, G., OZBILGIN, M.F. and WORMAN, D. (2005)

Managing diversity: linking theory and practice to business performance. Change agenda. London: CIPD.

MULHOLLAND, G., OZBILGIN, M.F. and WORMAN, D. (2006)

Managing diversity: words into actions. Executive briefing. London: CIPD.

OZBILGIN, M.F. TATLI, A. and WORMAN, D. (2007)

Managing diversity in practice: supporting business goals. Research into practice report. London: CIPD.

TATLI, A., OZBILGIN, M.F. and WORMAN, D. (2006)

Managing diversity: measuring success. Change agenda. London: CIPD.

THOMAS TAYLOR, W., PIASECKA, A. and WORMAN, D. (2005)

Managing diversity: learning by doing. Change agenda. London: CIPD.

WORMAN, D., BLAND, A. and CHASE, P. (2005)

Managing diversity: people make the difference at work – but everyone is different. Guide. London: CIPD.

OTHER REFERENCES

ASHFORTH, B.E. and MAEL, F. (1989)

Social identity theory and the organization. *Academy of Management Review.* Vol 14, No 1. January. pp20–39.

BARKEMA, H.G., BAUM, J. and MANNIX, E. (2002)

Management challenges in a new time. *Academy of Management Journal.* Vol 45, No 5, October. pp916–930.

CASSELL, C. and BISWAS, R. (2000)

Managing diversity in the new millennium. *Personnel Review.* Vol 29, No 3, pp.268–273.

CHOO, C.W. (1998)

The knowing organization: how organizations use information to construct meaning, create knowledge, and make decisions. New York: Oxford University Press.

COCKBURN, C. (1991)

In the way of women: men's resistance to sex equality in organizations. Ithaca, NY: ILR Press.

COX, T.H. (1993)

Cultural diversity in organizations: theory, research and practice. San Francisco, CA: Berrett-Koehler.

COX, T.H. and BLAKE, S. (1991)

Managing cultural diversity: implications for organizational competitiveness. *Academy of Management Executive.* Vol 5, No 3, August. pp45–56.

CUMMINGS, J.N. (2004)

Work groups, structural diversity and knowledge sharing in a global organization. *Management Science.* Vol 50, No 3, March. pp352–364.

DADFAR, H. and GUSTAVSSON, P. (1992)

Competition by effective management of cultural diversity. *International Studies of Management and Organization*. Vol 22, No 4, Winter. pp81–92.

FERNANDEZ, J.P. (1991)

Managing a diverse work force: regaining the competitive edge. Lexington, MA: Lexington Books.

GOVINDARAJAN, V. and GUPTA, A.K. (2001)

Building an effective global business team. *MIT Sloan Management Review*. Vol 42, No 4, Summer. pp 63–71.

HITT, F. (1998)

Difficulties in the articulation of different representations linked to the concept of function. *Journal of Mathematical Behavior*. Vol 17, No 1. pp123–134.

HOPKINS, W.E. and HOPKINS, S.A. (2002)

Effects of cultural recomposition on group interaction processes. *Academy of Management Review*. Vol 27, No 4, October. pp541–553.

JONES, R.T., JERICH, B., COPELAND, L. AND BOYLE, M. (1989)

Four by Four: how do you manage a diverse workforce. *Training and Development Journal*. Vol 43. No 2, pp 13–21.

KIDDER, D.L., LANKAU, M.J. and CHROBOT-MASON, D. (2004)

Backlash towards diversity initiatives: examining the impact of diversity program justification, personal and group outcomes. *International Journal of Conflict Management*. Vol 15, No 1. pp77–102.

LARKEY, L.K. (1996)

Toward a theory of communicative interactions in culturally diverse workgroups. *Academy of Management Review*. Vol 21, No 2,April. pp463–491.

LAWRENCE, E. (2000)

Equal opportunities officers and managing equality changes, *Personnel Review*. Vol 29. No 3, pp 381–401.

LEONARD-BARTON, D. (1995)

Wellsprings of knowledge: building and sustaining the sources of innovation., Boston, MA: Harvard Business School Press.

MCDOUGALL, M. (1996)

Equal opportunities versus managing diversity: another challenge for public sector management? *International Journal of Public Sector Management*.Vol. 9, No 5/6, pp 62–72.

MALFROY, J. (2002)

Intersecting worlds: inherent tensions and new practices in doctoral study. *Proceedings of the Fourth International Biennial Conference on Professional Doctorates*. Brisbane: Queensland University of Technology. Paper submitted 29 September 2002 (unpublished).

MANNIX, E. (2003)

Editor's comments: conflict and conflict resolution – a return to theorizing. *Academy of Management Review*. Vol 28, No 4, October. pp543–546.

MEYERSON, D.E. (2001)

Tempered radicals: how people use difference to inspire change at work. Boston, MA: Harvard Business School Press.

NONAKA, I. and TAKEUCHI, H. (1995)

The knowledge-creating company: how Japanese companies create the dynamics of innovation. Oxford: Oxford University Press.

OZBILGIN, M.F. and TATLI, A. (2008)

Global diversity management: an evidence based approach. London and New York: Palgrave.

PARKER, C. (1999)

How to win hearts and minds: corporate compliance policies for sexual harassment. *Law and Policy*. Vol 21,No 1, pp 21–48.

RAATIKAINEN, P. (2002)

Contributions of multiculturalism to the competitive advantage of an organization. *Singapore Management Review*. Vol 24, No 1. pp81–88.

REASON, P. and BRADBURY, H. (2001)

Handbook of action research: participative inquiry and practice. London: Sage.

SVYANTEK, D.J., MAHONEY, K.T. and BROWN, L.L. (2002)

Diversity and effectiveness in the Roman and Persian empires. *International Journal of Organizational Analysis*. Vol 10, No 3. pp260–283.

THOMAS, K.W. and TYMON, W.G. (1982)

Necessary properties of relevant research: lessons from recent criticisms of the organizational sciences. *Academy of Management Review*. Vol 7, No 3, July. pp345–352.

THOMAS, R.R. (1990)

From affirmative action to affirming diversity, *Harvard BusinessReview*. Vol. 68, no 2. pp 107–17.

TRANFIELD, D. and STARKEY, K. (1998)

The nature, social organization and promotion of management research: towards policy. *British Journal of Management*. Vol 9, No 4, December. pp341–353.

WATSON, W. E., KUMAR, K. and MICHAELSEN, L. K. (1993).

Cultural diversity's impact on interaction process and performance: comparing homogeneous and diverse task groups. *Academy of Management Journal*. Vol 36, No 3, June. pp590–602.

WEICK, K.E. (1995)

Sensemaking in organizations. Thousand Oaks, CA: Sage.